CW00688622

AFGHAN FACES

AFGHAN FACES

JOHN CASSON

All profits from the sale of this book will be donated to UK charities that support members of our armed forces injured in Afghanistan and Sandy Gall's Afghanistan Appeal

www.afghanfaces.co.uk

First published in the UK in 2010 by John Casson
www.johncasson.com

Hollowcombe, Start Point, Nr Kingsbridge, Devon, UK, TQ7 2NF

© John Casson 2010

Photographs © Jeremy Rata 2010

Map © MAPS IN MINUTES™/Geo-Innovations 2010

A CIP catalogue record of this book is available from the British Library.

ISBN 978-0-9566998-0-0

Designed by Craig Stevens
www.craig-stevens.co.uk

Printed and bound in the UK
by Butler Tanner & Dennis
www.butlertanneranddennis.com

CARING FOR THE ENVIRONMENT

This book was printed in the UK by Butler Tanner & Dennis, saving the environmental
cost of long distance transportation to major markets. The printing facility has all
its operations under one roof and employs mainly local people, many cycling to work.
It is certified to ISO 14001 and is aiming to soon achieve carbon neutrality. It was
printed using 100% vegetable-based inks on Respecta Silk FSC paper. Respecta Silk
is produced from 100% Elemental Chlorine Free (EFC) pulp that is fully recyclable.
It has a Forest Stewardship Council (FSC) accreditation and is produced by a mill
which supports well-managed forestry schemes.

To all those who have suffered as a result of conflict in Afghanistan

Foreword

When I first started travelling in Afghanistan in 1982 – I had been there briefly in 1975 – I was struck by the remarkable purity of the air. There was no pollution, because there was no industry and very few cars, so no diesel fumes. That was the third year of the Russian occupation and I had gone there with the Mujahideen to make the first of three documentaries about the war.

In those days, you had to walk everywhere or ride a horse. I was a few years younger then, so the team and I got very fit – and thinner. I think I lost a stone and a half and I wasn't fat to start with. But the point of this story is to explain that I took better photographs than any I'd taken before – it was undoubtedly to do with the clear air. So, if a bad photographer like me could take good photographs in Afghanistan, just think of what can we expect from a Jeremy Rata. He is a superb photographer even in the often murky light of the West Country, but in the clarity of the Hindu Kush we can expect something exceptional, and I am delighted to tell you he has excelled himself.

Both the author John Casson and Jeremy Rata have combined in a fascinating enterprise to bring Afghanistan and its variety of tribes and peoples, from Aimaqs, Uzbeks and Hazaras – who some say are descended from Genghis Khan's armies – to Persian-speaking Tajiks and the largest minority of all, the Pushtuns, into sharp focus. Despite the horrors of the war against the Taliban, in which the British, the Americans and the rest of NATO have now been engaged for nine years, Afghanistan is still a beautiful country, with spectacular mountains, rivers and lakes, a history that goes back to Alexander the Great and early Buddhism, two periods which cross-fertilised one another to produce the great art of Gandhara. The magic of Jeremy Rata's wonderful collection of photographs brings the whole romantic and turbulent story into the present, showing us the people of Afghanistan as they are today.

John Casson's contribution has been beyond all praise. *Afghan Faces* is his idea, from start to finish, motivated by the desire to raise substantial funds for British armed forces' charities and for my Afghanistan Appeal.

It is also based, very importantly, on his friendship with Jeremy, whose brave decision it was to take part in what at times must have seemed a hazardous enterprise. John has financed this whole venture himself, the book and the expedition. He hopes, and we all hope that *Afghan Faces* will be the great success it deserves to be.

Eleanor, as UK Director of Sandy Gall's Afghanistan Appeal, and I as Chairman, and all our Committee, who have been working for the disabled of Afghanistan since 1983, are deeply grateful for their generosity and hard work.

'Tashakor,' 'Thank you,' as our Afghan friends would say.

Sandy Gall

Introduction

Although I have had a lifelong interest in international news and world affairs, I had not been to Afghanistan until I went on a visit organised by Sandy Gall two years ago. I vividly remember watching his reports on ITN's *News at Ten* during the Russian occupation but never thought for a moment that one day I would have the opportunity of travelling with him.

On that trip, which included a short stay in Kabul and several days in Bamiyan, I found the Afghans I met friendly, largely misunderstood by the outside world and, above all, photogenic. I concluded that most of them desperately wanted an end to war and destruction and the opportunity to live in peace. The following year I met Jeremy Rata, an award-wining hotelier and professional photographer, who was fascinated by my stories about Afghanistan. When I suggested that we go there together on a photographic expedition, which would lead to a book, he immediately agreed.

We left in August for Kabul, the capital of Afghanistan, on what was to prove a difficult and challenging visit and not without incident! With its hundreds of gun-toting security guards, razor wire, sandbagged and fortified areas around embassies, government buildings and banks, one was aware of the constant threat of terrorist attack. We were somewhat reassured, however, by the many Afghan army and police checkpoints.

We drove, with a fearsome-looking armed guard, from Kabul to Jalalabad and the Pakistan border, on one of the busiest roads in the country, described by the BBC as 'the most dangerous road in the world,' not so much because of the Taliban but thanks to reckless driving, the cause of many serious accidents. On the surface, Jalalabad seemed to be untouched by the insurgency yet, as we went round the city, we were told the Taliban had banned the sale of TV sets and DVDs. We did not see any, in fact, so the death threats appeared to be taken seriously, with Taliban intimidation undermining the authority of the government. A low-flying unmanned spy plane (drone) operated by somebody behind a desk in the USA flew ominously overhead.

Our next stop, Bamiyan, the centre of Afghanistan's Hazara minority, was famous for two giant Buddhas, dating from the sixth century – the older, Small Buddha 115 feet (28 metres) high and the later Large Buddha, 174 feet (35 metres). They once stood carved into the side of a mountain. I say 'once stood' for in March 2001 they were destroyed by extremist elements in the Taliban.

Jeremy Rata

In the 1960s and 1970s Bamiyan, like the rest of Afghanistan, was on the hippy trail to India. Its spectacular valleys and dramatic mountains, some surmounted by the ruins of ancient fortresses, became a celebrated tourist destination. Because of the past and despite the slaughter they have suffered at the hands of the Taliban, local people still welcome visitors with a warm smile.

Our last destination was the historic city of Herat, in the west near the Iranian border, where we found a very different atmosphere. Once a thriving oasis on the Silk Road this hot, humid and windy city feels alive and vibrant. Its inhabitants happily greet us and are very obliging when the camera appears. Only a few hours before our arrival, a suicide bomber had blown up two petrol tankers at the side of the airport road, killing four people. We saw their funeral cortege of four minibuses slowly winding its way round the old city.

Wherever you go in Afghanistan the shops are well stocked, the markets busy, the majority of goods imported from Iran, Pakistan and above all, China. The Afghans' long history of war and invasion has made them fiercely independent and proud. The family is all-important, and family honour paramount. For the vast majority of Afghans, life is hard which makes them frugal and industrious. And because of war and deprivation, there are many limbless and disabled, although not only as a result of war. Club foot is common and the effects of polio are still very much in evidence.

The photographs in this book were selected from well over a thousand taken during our 12-day visit as we explored the cities, towns, villages and countryside. The Afghans made a very definite and positive impression on me and I think they are worthy of our support.

After the cost of the printing of *Afghan Faces*, the profits will be donated to UK charities that support members of our armed forces injured in Afghanistan and to Sandy Gall's Afghanistan Appeal. For further information regarding donations and to purchase *Afghan Faces* online, please visit **www.afghanfaces.co.uk**

Thank you for your support

John Casson

John Casson

Thanks

Thank you to Bob Pennington, Covert Protection Limited (www.covertprotection.com), former Assistant Chief Constable Devon & Cornwall Police, who was responsible for organising and overseeing the complex security arrangements for John Casson and Jeremy Rata's visit to Afghanistan in August 2010.

Thank you also to Muqim Jamshady, Afghan Logistics & Tours Pvt. Co. Ltd (www.afghanlogisticstours.com), his drivers Wahid and Najeeb and security guard Shareen for taking such good care of them while they were in the country.

Afghanistan

PHOTOGRAPHS

Pause for a photograph, Afghan men
are very photogenic

Herat

Amused at being caught asleep

Herat Citadel

Smithy

Backstreets of Bamiyan

Morning ritual

Bamiyan

Traders

Spice market, Herat

A typical police patrol, always a favoured target for the Taliban

Herat

Bullets

Police patrol vehicle, Bamiyan

The imposing Darul Aman Palace on the outskirts of
Kabul was built in the early 1920s by King Amanullah Khan.
Gutted by fire in 1969, it was restored and used by the Afghan
Defence Ministry during the 1970s and 1980s. In 1992, after
the withdrawal of the Russian occupation, the Mujahideen
bombarded it into the sad condition it is in today

Mealtime, shepherds taking a well-earned rest
on their way to Kabul, nine days still to go

Bamiyan Valley

Like so many others, a sad face

Bamiyan

Earning its keep

Bamiyan

In full flight. The striking blue burqa has been traditional
for women in Afghanistan since long before the Taliban

Jalalabad

A lot of love and care is given to these special needs children, not only by their families but also by the Swedish Committee for Afghanistan who run this daily street clinic

Jalalabad

On call to the well-heeled

Herat airport

Birdcages

Ka Faroshi bird market, Kabul

Midday sun

Street market, Kabul

This boy would be too young to have experienced the horror of the Taliban visit to his village in 1998. The three remaining men were murdered just because they were Hazara. His family, like thousands of others, fled into the mountains just in time

Qala-e Dokhtar, Bamiyan Valley

Preparing for lunch

Bazaar, Bamiyan

———————————

Foundry, of all places, in Ka Faroshi bird market

Kabul

Moneychanger: while Afghanistan has its own
currency, the Afghani, the US dollar is king

A street corner near the British Embassy, Kabul

Helping grandad

Bazaar, Bamiyan

Still a long, long way to go. Shepherds walk to market across country for weeks with their herds

Valley of the Dragon, Bamiyan

Cooling down on a very hot and humid day

Herat

'Which is yours?'

Main bazaar, Bamiyan

It caught his eye

Ka Faroshi bird market, Kabul

Many a story to tell

Bazaar, Bamiyan

Gulp!

Street market, Kabul

That important call

Herat airport

Serving the nation, Afghan National Police

Herat Citadel

Receiving instruction, Afghan National Army officer

Kabul

Buy an ice cream, watch TV for free

Tent, Bamiyan

Naturally happy

Jalalabad

New generation

Jalalabad

School's out, time for home

Kabul

Looking away

Intersection, Jalalabad

Open cemetery, below the walls of the Bala Hissar fort

Kabul

Caring shepherd

Near Bamiyan Valley

Excitement, photographed for the first time

Kakrak Valley, Bamiyan

Mates

Old city, Herat

Begging. The Kabul to Jalalabad road, a lifeline
between Afghanistan and Pakistan, is the site
of daily attacks by the Taliban

Near Chakharbagy-Safa

A river in flood. It is very unusual for this region to experience rain in August, these floods were caused by the same torrential rain that affected Pakistan so badly in 2010

Bamiyan

Timepiece

Bazaar, Bamiyan

It's my turn. The Swedish Committee for Afghanistan
organise several community clinics in Jalalabad to help
the many disabled children, this child with spina bifida

Time on his side, the world passes by

Bamiyan

Hoping for sweets

Shahr-e Zohak, entrance to the Bamiyan Valley

How old? He says 90 plus. Behind him? No idea

Curator, Kabul museum

'What shall I to do next'

Old city, Herat

A landmine victim of the Afghan conflict,
both physically and mentally

Sandy Gall's Afghanistan Appeal, Jalalabad hospital

Almost there

Bazaar, Bamiyan

Late again

A backstreet in Herat

'A bird in the hand is worth two...'

Ka Faroshi bird market, Kabul

Waiting room

Sandy Gall's Afghanistan Appeal, Jalalabad hospital

Team effort

Spice market, Herat

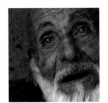

Chain shop

Old city, Herat

Flight attendant

Herat airport

Whose tank? It is not unusual to see abandoned
tanks on the road, many changed 'ownership'
during various conflicts

Police checkpoint, Bamiyan to Shar-e Zohak road, Bamiyan

Has he seen it?

Valley of the Dragon, Bamiyan

Will they win? Only time will tell.
Officer, Afghan National Army

Kabul

Darul Aman Palace, bombarded by the Mujahideen

Kabul

Darul Aman Palace, needless destruction

Kabul

Thousand-yard stare

Sandy Gall's Afghanistan Appeal, Jalalabad hospital

What next?

Sandy Gall's Afghanistan Appeal, Jalalabad hospital

How did this happen to me?

Sandy Gall's Afghanistan Appeal, Jalalabad hospital

This young man was a soldier with the Afghan
National Army until a few months earlier when
he stood on a landmine. Standing around him,
just as traumatised, are his brothers

Sandy Gall's Afghanistan Appeal, Jalalabad hospital

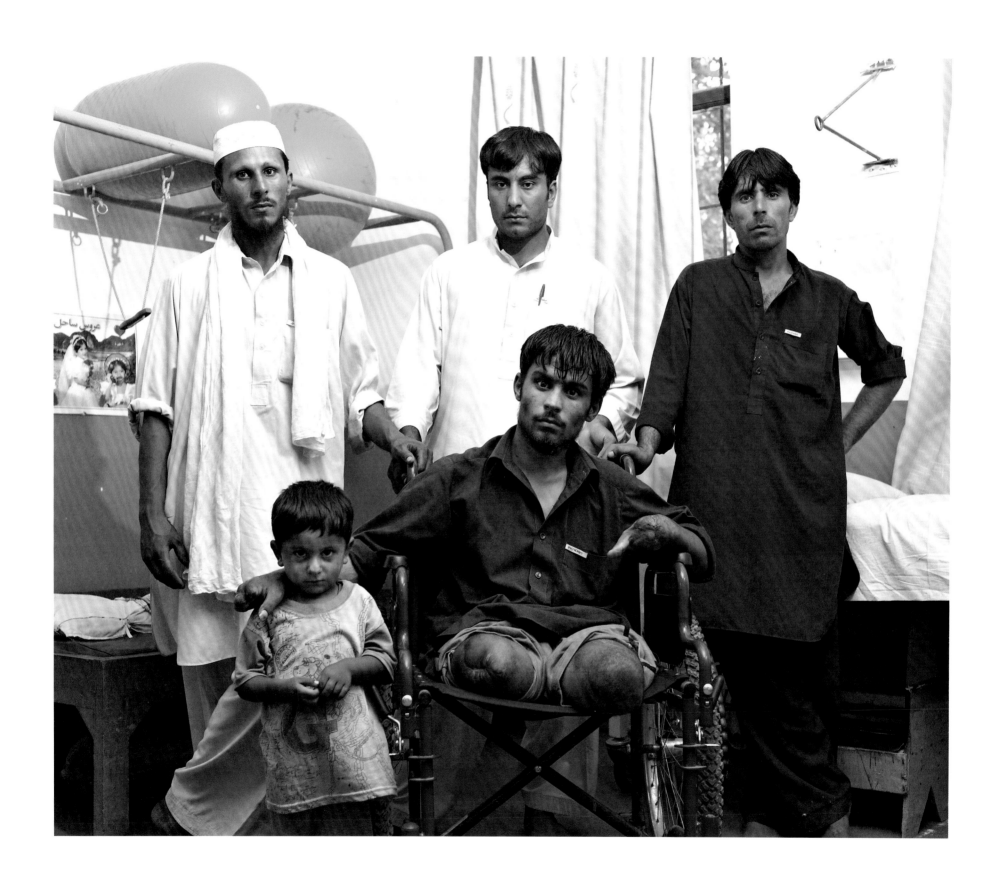

Heavy load

Bamiyan

Who gets the bird?

Ka Faroshi bird market, Kabul

Kindly face in the rabbit shop

Ka Faroshi bird market, Kabul

Coping with old age, begging on the street, not such
a common sight as in other Asian countries

Old city, Herat

Many babies in the Nangarhar region of Afghanistan, near
the Pakistan border, are born with club foot. The pioneering
non-surgical Ponseti treatment introduced to Afghanistan
by Sandy Gall's Afghanistan Appeal has successfully
corrected this condition for thousands of babies

Jalalabad hospital

AFGHAN FACES

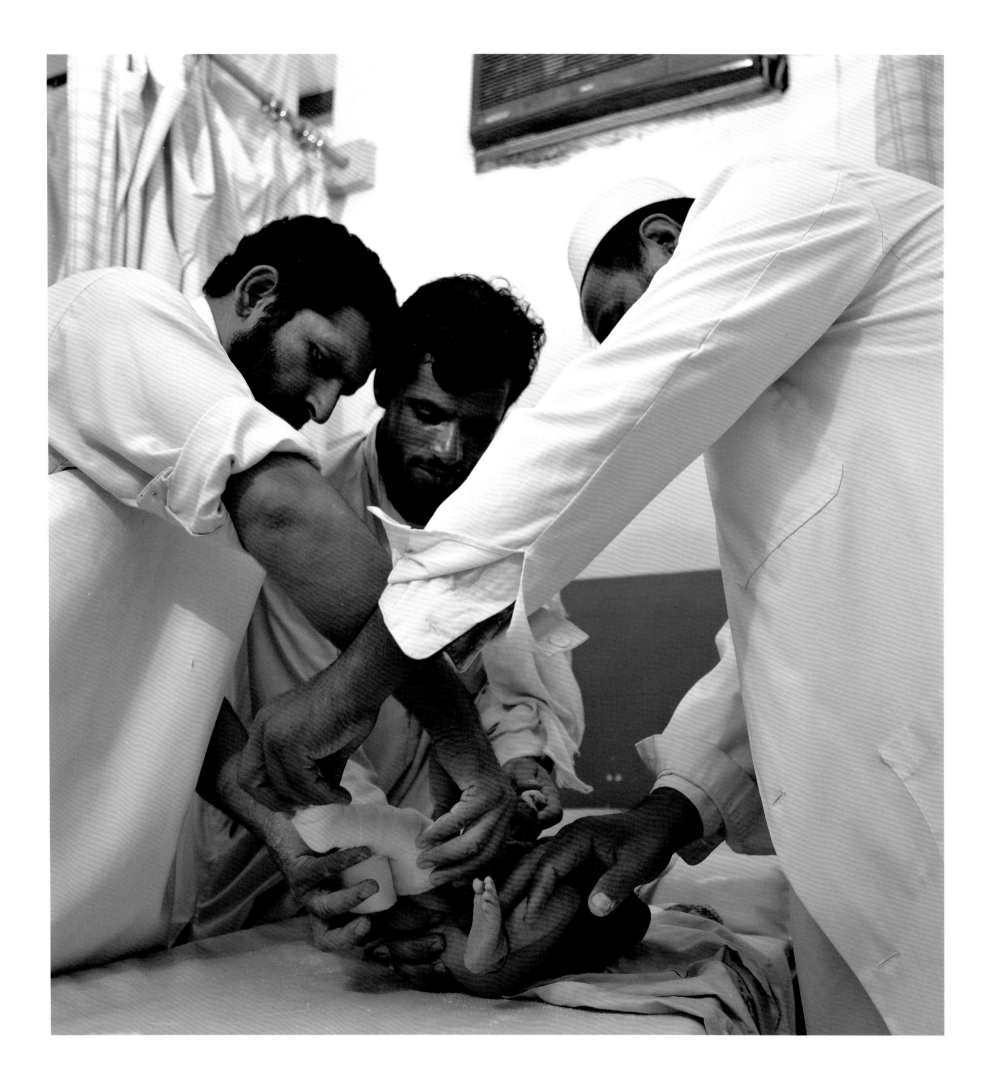

Thirsty work

Bakery, Herat

A victim of post-polio paralysis, this man is one
of the 20 per cent of disabled employees who work
for Sandy Gall's Afghanistan Appeal workshop
at Jalalabad hospital, which makes artificial feet,
wheelchairs and crutches

Watching and learning

Market in Kabul

Earning pocket money

Qala-e Dokhtar, Bamiyan

Brushes, brushes and more brushes

Herat

Men on a mission

Shahr-e Zohak to Bamiyan road

On the way to market

Near Shahr-e Zohak, entrance to the Bamiyan Valley

Butcher's shop

Jalalabad

Afghani naan bread being made in the traditional way

Bazaar, Bamiyan

Reflective – maybe reliving the horror of his injuries.
This Afghan soldier, victim of a landmine, is waiting
for treatment

Kabul Orthopaedic Organisation clinic

This resigned little boy was spending months with his
brother herding goats across the country, he had not
seen his mother for two years

Valley of the Dragon, Bamiyan

'Are we next?'

Street market, Kabul

Sacred entrance

Kakrak Valley, Bamiyan

Until puberty, young Afghan girls generally
do not cover their faces

Jalalabad

Chastisement

Police post, Bamiyan

'The Kite Runner'

On the road past the Russian Embassy, Kabul

Missed appointment

Jalalabad

Ouch!

Sandy Gall's Afghanistan Appeal, Jalalabad hospital

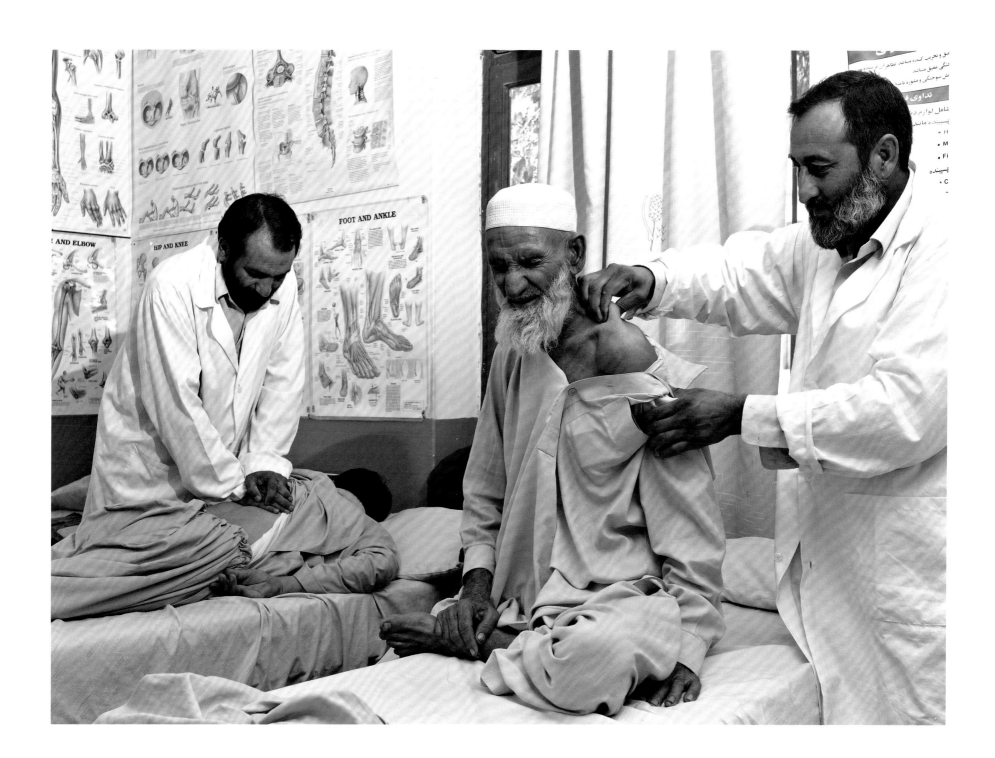

End of the day

Herat

Making it comfortable, a landmine victim
with his prosthetic leg

Sandy Gall's Afghanistan Appeal, Jalalabad hospital

Having fun, the child is only wearing the burqa for playtime,
not for any cultural or religious reason

Backstreets of Jalalabad

A typical sight around government,
embassy and military installations

Kabul

Bujal Bazi, a traditional game played by Afghan children

Bamiyan Valley

Jewellers, one of many

Herat

_____

'Who's there?'

Spice market, old city, Herat

Has the treatment worked? Probably, the success rate
is very high. This baby is receiving the non-clinical
Ponseti treatment for club foot

Sandy Gall's Afghanistan Appeal, Jalalabad hospital

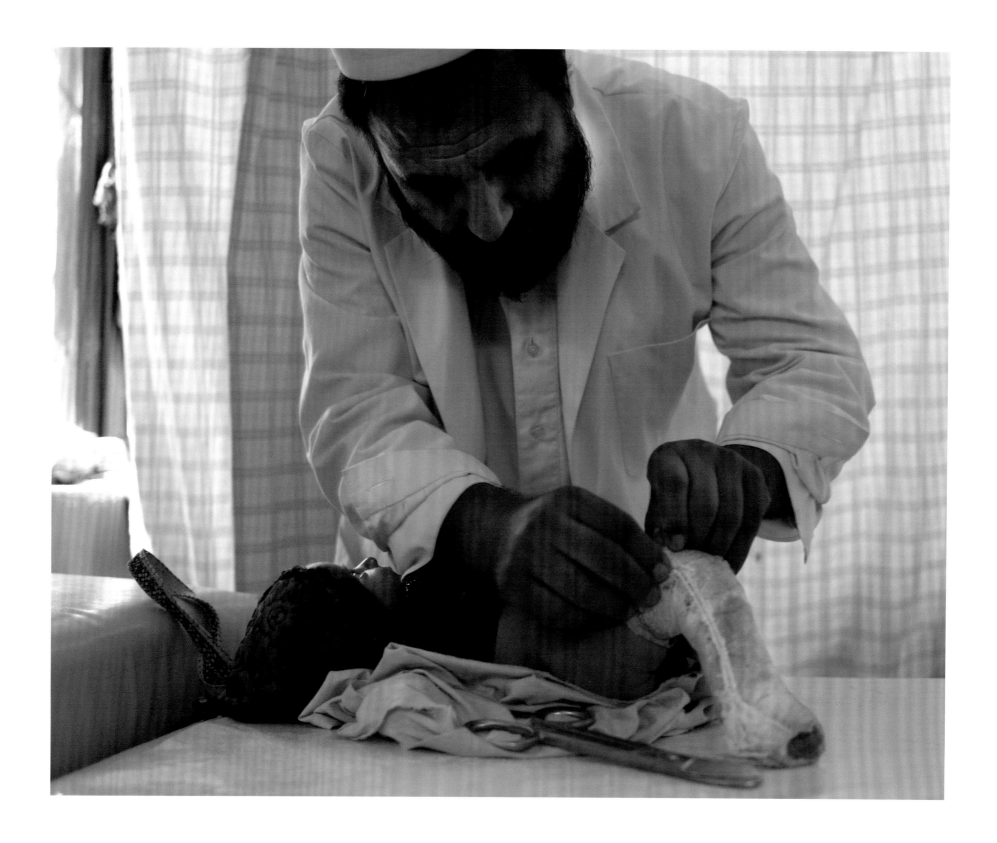

Polio is very common in Afghanistan

Sandy Gall's Afghanistan Appeal, Jalalabad hospital

This young man is probably no more than 18 years old
(dates of birth are not recorded in many parts of Afghanistan).
An Afghan soldier, he stepped on a landmine three months
earlier in Kandahar. Unusually for landmine victims who are
badly traumatised, he smiled and appeared very relaxed

Kabul Orthopaedic Organisation clinic, Military hospital

Visiting soldiers

Kabul museum

AFGHAN FACES

AFGHAN FACES

This young man is probably no more than 18 years old
(dates of birth are not recorded in many parts of Afghanistan).
An Afghan soldier, he stepped on a landmine three months
earlier in Kandahar. Unusually for landmine victims who are
badly traumatised, he smiled and appeared very relaxed

Kabul Orthopaedic Organisation clinic, Military hospital

Watch

Jalalabad

Receiving treatment for a genetic spinal condition

Kabul Orthopaedic Organisation clinic

'You look kindly at me; I look kindly at you'

Sandy Gall's Afghanistan Appeal, Jalalabad hospital

The country's future

Backstreets of Herat

Sweet dreams

Old city, Herat

Outpatient day

Sandy Gall's Afghanistan Appeal, Jalalabad hospital

In a world of his own, earning a living

Herat

_____

Kandahari man's livelihood

Herat

_____

Firewood

Outskirts of Kabul

Always vigilant

Kakrak Valley, Bamiyan

Young shopkeeper

Backstreets of Jalalabad

Help in society. This man, who has received treatment
for polio, has also had help from the Swedish Committee
for Afghanistan to set up a small street stall selling
drinks and snacks as part of a community occupational
therapy project

Backstreets of Jalalabad

Afghan soldier waiting for treatment

Kabul Orthopaedic Organisation clinic

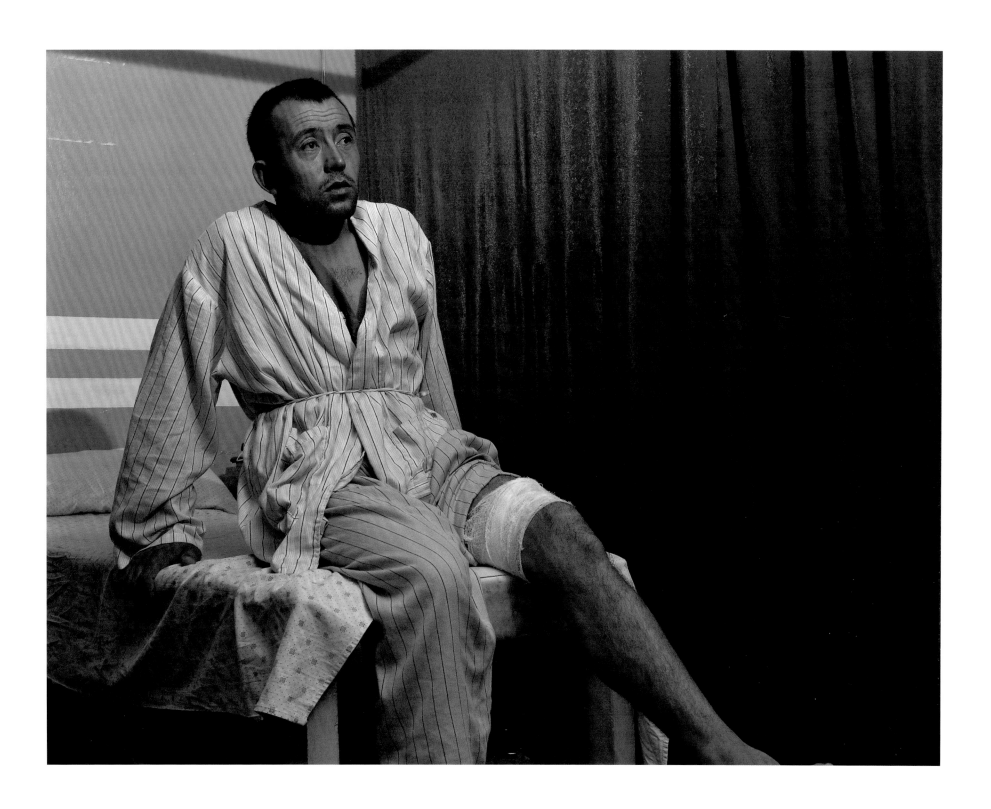

Leprosy

Old market, Herat

Showing respect to their religion and ethnic background,
Afghan men wear some form of headdress

Bamiyan

A father's care

Sandy Gall's Afghanistan Appeal, Jalalabad hospital

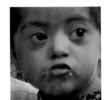

The family is an important institution
for the Afghan people

Jalalabad

Young girl

Jalalabad

A victim of a landmine blast that left him blind in one
eye and with no legs, this man gets on with life and
works for Sandy Gall's Afghanistan Appeal workshop
at Jalalabad hospital

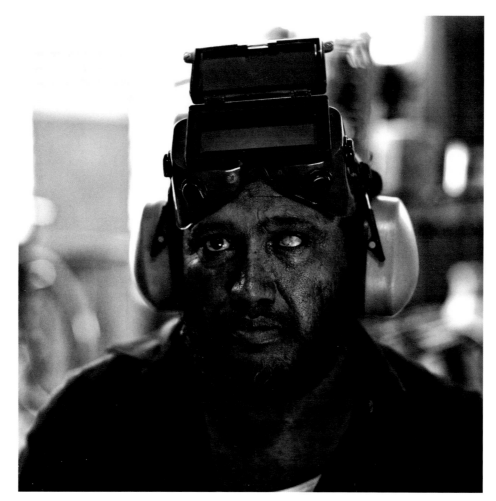

No Afghan faces to be found here, this is the scene
of a suicide attack that took place a few hours earlier.
The bomber and four innocent people were killed

Airport road, Herat

Fagin's brother?

Ka Faroshi bird market, Kabul

Afghanistan has probably the highest number of crutches
per population of any country worldwide, yet there are still
nowhere near enough to meet demand. These crutches
are made at Sandy Gall's Afghanistan Appeal workshop

Jalalabad hospital

Labour of love

Sandy Gall's Afghanistan Appeal clinic, Jalalabad hospital

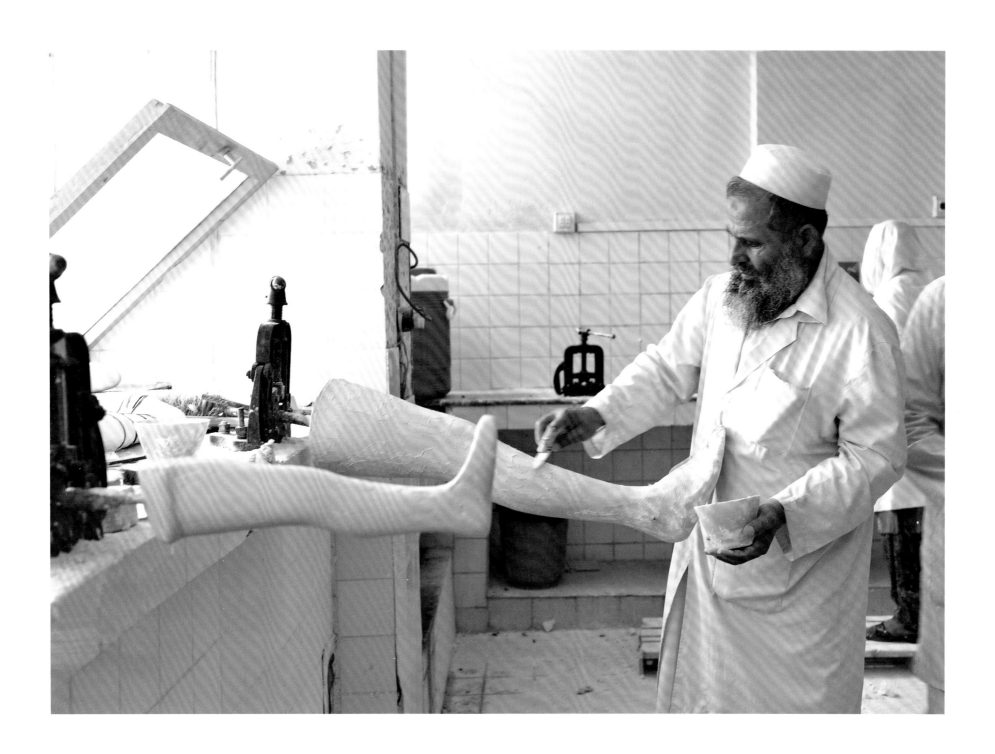

The author's fearless Pashtun bodyguard

Valley of the Dragon, Bamiyan

'One day, Father'

Kakrak Valley, Bamiyan

These children attend a regular special needs clinic
(often in no more than a corner of a courtyard or
on the balcony of a small office complex) run by
the Swedish Committee for Afghanistan

Jalalabad